With our songs in your heart
(And your cash in our pocket!)
You can now carry this book
(Even tho you can't carry a tune!)
And...

SING ALONG WITH
MAD

Just don't be surprised if the
world turns a deaf ear!

More **MAD** Humor from **SIGNET**

SING ALONG WITH

WITH

by Frank Jacobs

Illustrated by Al Jaffee

Edited by Albert B. Feldstein

with a Foreword by Nick Meglin

A SIGNET BOOK from

NEW AMERICAN LIBRARY

TIMES MIRROR

New York and Scarborough, Ontario
The New English Library Limited, London

SIGNET, SIGNET CLASSICS, MENTOR, PLUME AND MERIDIAN BOOKS
are published *in the United States* by
The New American Library, Inc.,
1301 Avenue of the Americas, New York, New York 10019,
in Canada by The New American Library of Canada Limited,
81 Mack Avenue, Scarborough, 704, Ontario,
in the United Kingdom by The New English Library Limited,
Barnard's Inn, Holborn, London, E.C. 1, England

FIRST PRINTING, NOVEMBER, 1970

7 8 9 10 11 12 13

PRINTED IN THE UNITED STATES OF AMERICA

FOREWORD

It has been said that forewords for books are pointless, meaningless, and boring. Some of the people who *say* these things are pointless, meaningless, and boring! But they are also RIGHT!

Except for this *one time!*

For this is no *ordinary* pointless, meaningless, and boring foreword—this is a CHAIN foreword!

All you have to do to avoid breaking the chain is to buy two (2) *more* copies of this book, sign the foreword pages of all three (3) copies and mail them to three (3) of your friends. They each in turn buy three (3) copies of this book, sign the foreword pages, and mail them to three (3) of *their* friends. Someone just might make thousands of dollars from this chain. On the other hand, one (1) reader, Omar Keslo of South Bergen, New Jersey, *broke* the chain and died!

The decision to participate in this wonderful chain is completely voluntary and is yours alone to make. Just don't say you haven't been warned about Omar Keslo!

nick meglin

Nick Meglin
Chain Editor
Mad Magazine

Contents

MY
SQUARE
LESTER

CAST OF CHARACTERS

Henry Headman, the
star-maker of the
Rock industry.

Pitkin, his
right-hand man.

Lester Doobetter,
a teen-age square.

Marigold Shapiro,
a tantalizing
teeny-bopper.

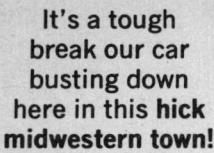

11

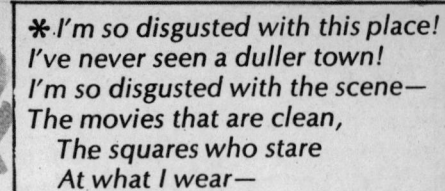

*Sung to the tune of
"I've Grown Accustomed To Her Face"

15

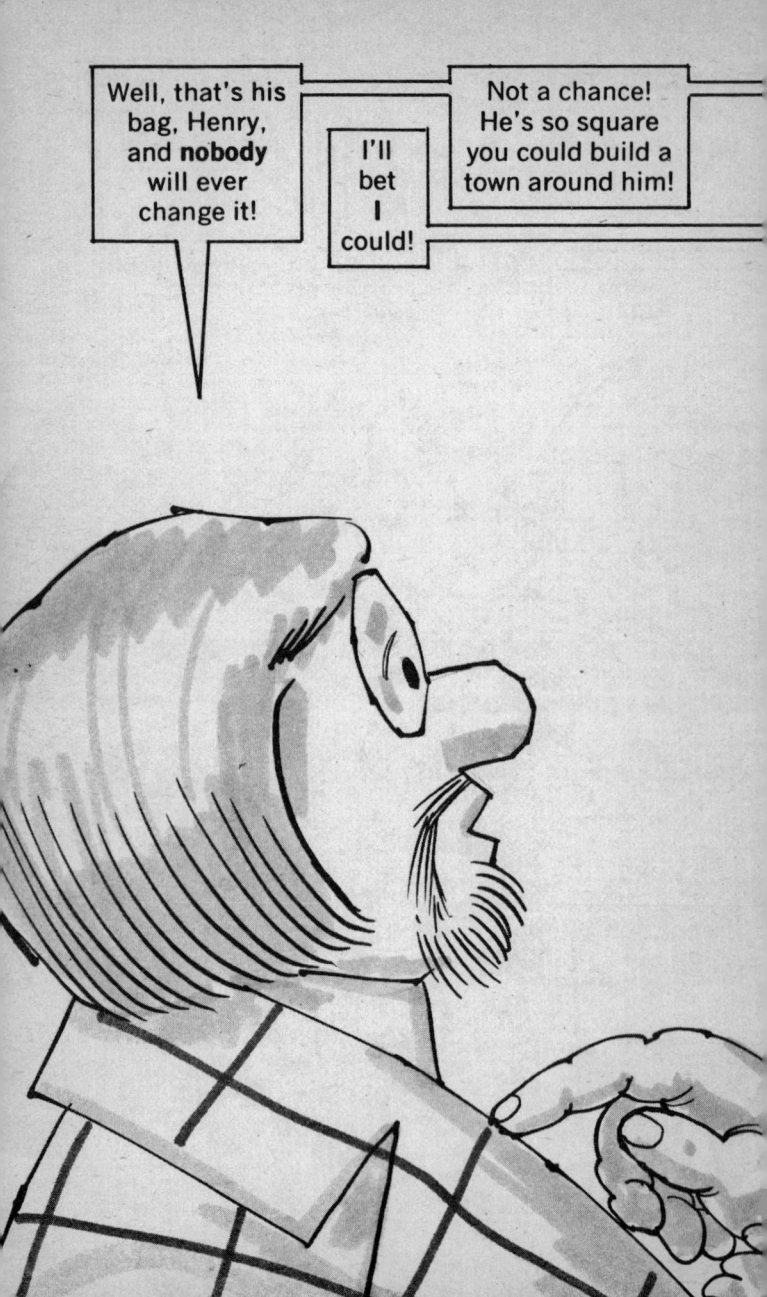

23

24

25

*Sung to the tune of "With a Little Bit of Luck"

Two weeks pass.
Lester, who has left
his square life in
his Midwestern home-town,
is living in
Henry Headman's New York
apartment, where he is
being transformed
into a full-fledged
rock star.

*Sung to the tune of "The Rain in Spain"

39

41

42

Then blast the pigs—
They'll flip their wigs on campus;
The kids will think you're out of sight;

And for your final bow,
Belt out a quote from Mao—
You'll wow your fans, fans, fans all night!

A month goes by.
After his smash debut
at the Poughkeepsie
Rock Festival,
Lester has emerged as
the top star in
the entire country,
with eleven of his albums
in the Top Ten.

47

*I have often walked from a job before,
But I never had to fight a female mob before!
   Now they pounce on me,
   'Cause, quite suddenly,
I'm the cat with the beat that they groove!

I can see that there's no escape for me!
It's quite clear this hungry mob
   is going ape for me!
   How they scream and swear
   As the clothes they tear
From the cat with the beat that they groove!

*Sung to the tune of "On The Street Where You Live"

50

*Sung to the tune of "Get Me To the Church on Time"

55

A SONG SALUTING THE UNITED STATES POST OFFICE

*Saturday . . .
I was mailed a letter Saturday
From a friend of mine three blocks away;
He sent it off . . . on Saturday;

Monday's mail . . .
Made me hopeful but to no avail;
Just a postcard for a clearance sale—
That's all there was . . . in Monday's mail;

Tuesday
Was . . . the . . . same;
All that came was just a bill;
Ev'ry
Day . . . I . . . look;
Like a schnook, I'm looking still;

One fine day . . .
When I'm ninety and my hair is gray,
I am certain it will come my way—
That letter mailed . . . last Saturday!

*Sung to the tune of "Yesterday"

ON-THE-JOB
LOVE
SONGS

The Businessman's Love Song
Sung to the tune of *"For Me and My Gal"*

Tax laws I'm breaking
    For me and my doll;
Deductions taking
    For me and my doll;

All my gifts I'm defraying
As expenses outlaying;
That's the reason I'm paying
    My accountant named Sol;

The Dentist's Love Song

Sung to the tune of
"Oh What a Beautiful Morning"

There's a bright silver cap on your cuspid;
There's a bright silver cap on your cuspid;
The gold glitters down
　　from your bridgework above —
One filling is loose and I'm falling in love!

69

The Waiter's Love Song

Sung to the tune of
"I Can't Give You Anything But Love"

I won't feed you anything but steak, baby!
Steak will never make your tummy ache, baby!
    Leg of lamb,
    Pork and ham,
They're not for you!
    Breast of veal —
    That's no meal!
Neither is a kidney stew!

Oh, you've got too much class for
    chicken pie, baby!
Plates of eggs for you I'll never fry, baby!
Just the thought of hash would
    make me cry, baby!
I won't feed you anything but steak!

The Optician's Love Song

Sung to the tune of
"I'm in Love With a Wonderful Guy"

I
AM
HOPING
YOU'LL READ
EVERY LINE HERE;
THOUGH THE PRINT GETS

SMALLER IN SIZE; THEN DEAREST

HEART, YOU WILL SEE FROM THIS CHART

I'M IN LOVE WITH YOUR NEAR-SIGHTED EYES!

The Garbageman's Love Song

Sung to the tune of "I'll Be Seeing You"

How romance abounds
In piles of coffee grounds;
I'll see our love increase
Through apple cores,
Through rancid grease;

I am missing you
While dropping steak bones on the street,
While egg-shells crunch beneath my feet;
How soon, my dearest, shall we meet?

I think of you with every trail
    of orange-peels that I strew —
I am dumping chicken fat
And I am missing you!

The Doctor's Love Song

**Sung to the tune of
*"You're the Top"***

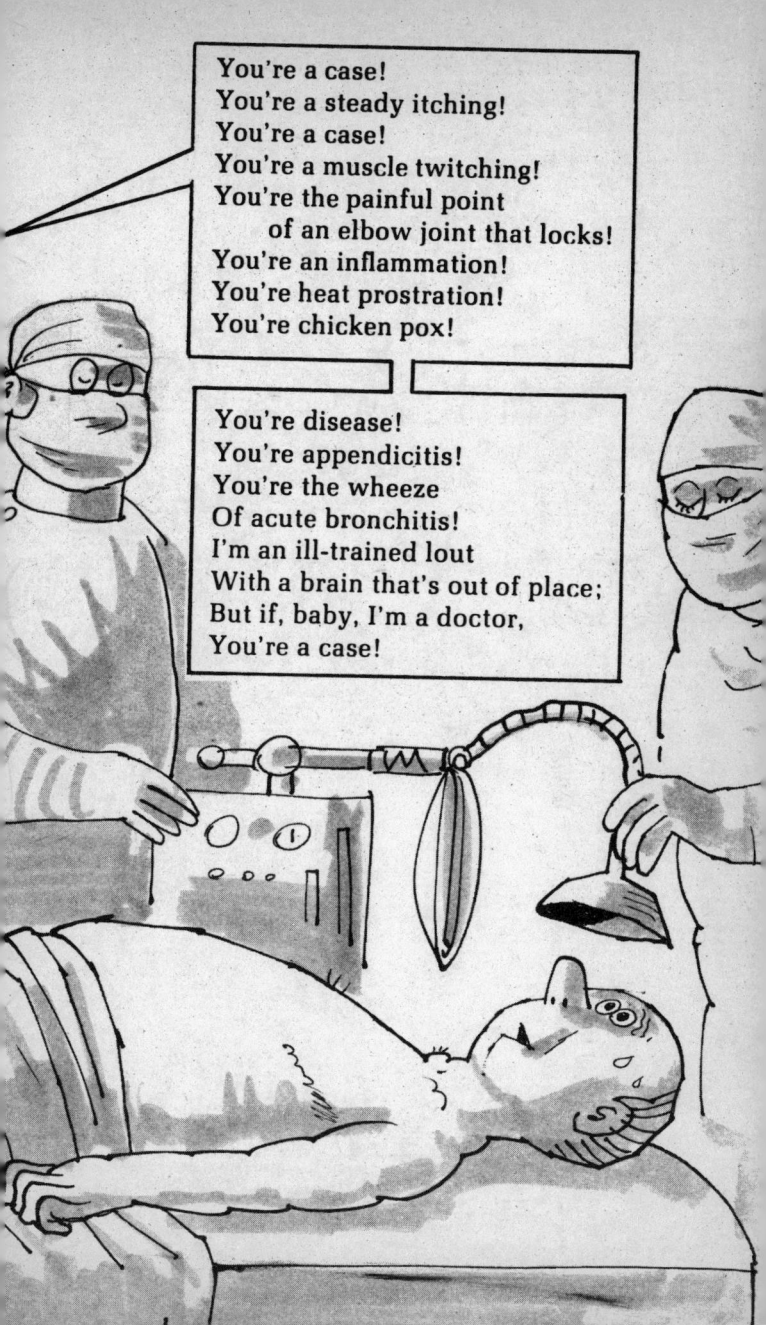

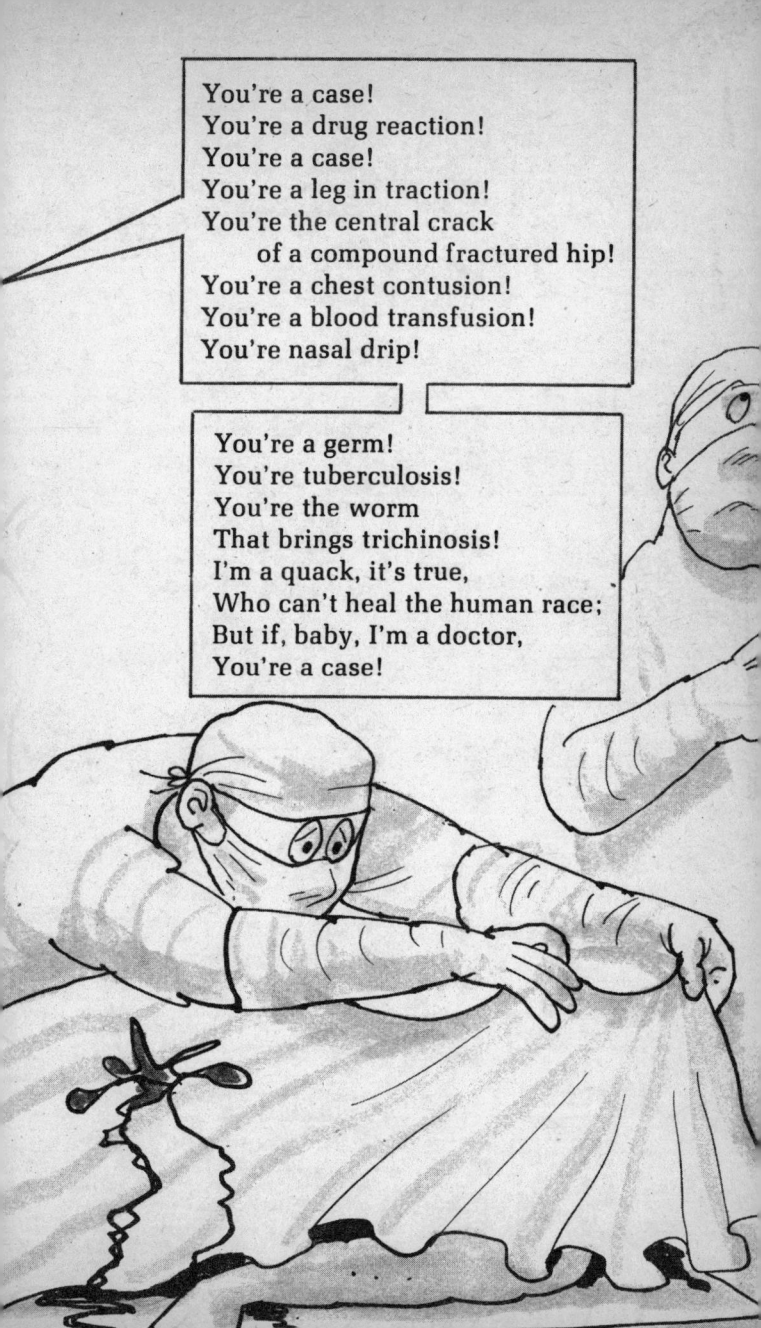

A SONG
TO BE SUNG
DURING A
POPULATION
EXPLOSION

*I'm bunched again—
I'm crunched again—
What's left of my body is hunched again—
Compressed, crowded and constricted
Am I!

I'm thin again—
Packed in again—
Squeezed in like sardines in a tin again—
Compressed, crowded and constricted
Am I!

See his crowd . . . overspilling—
    They're a cause . . . for alarm;
Ev'ry space they are filling,
    And I live . . . on . . . a . . . farm!

I ache again—
Bones break again—
I wish that the Pill folks would take again—
Compressed, crowded and constricted
Am I!

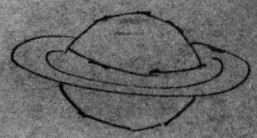

*Sung to the tune of "Bewitched,
    Bothered and Bewildered"

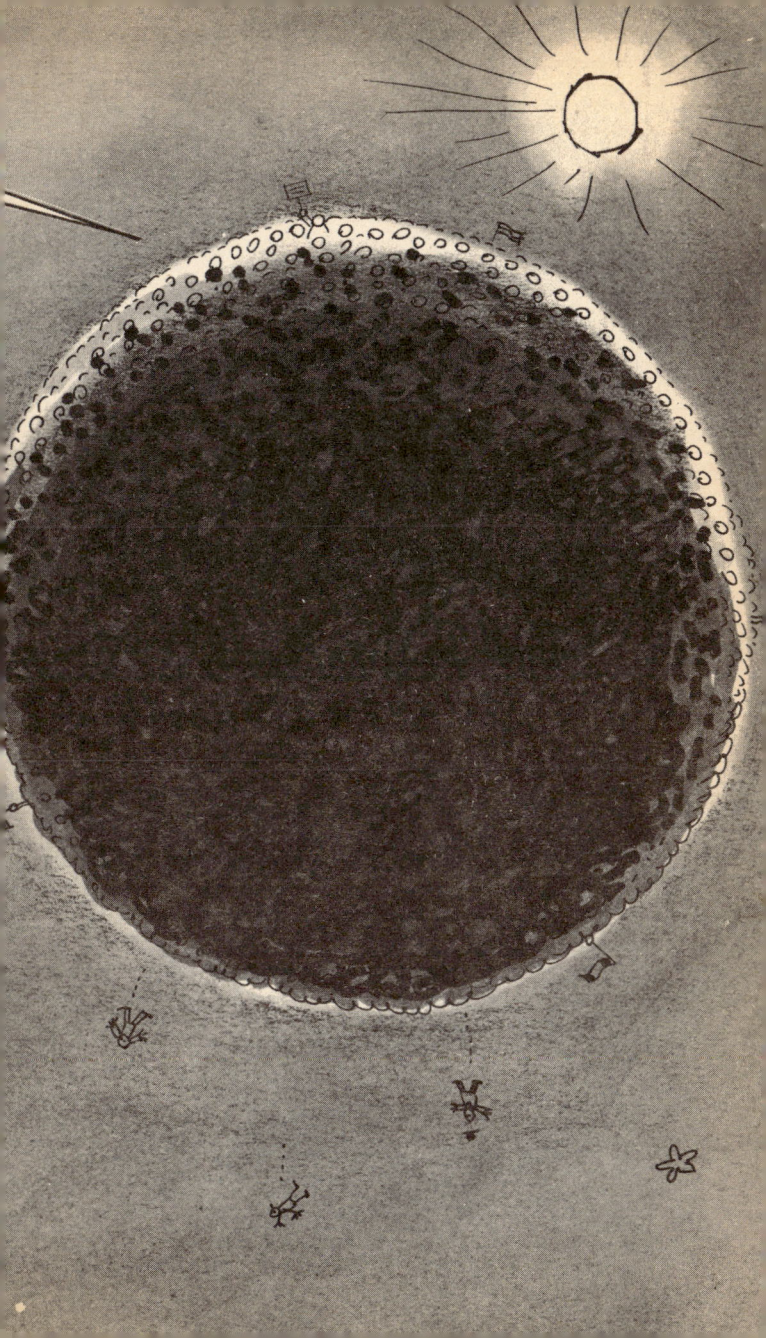

SONGS CELEBRATING GREAT HISTORICAL EVENTS

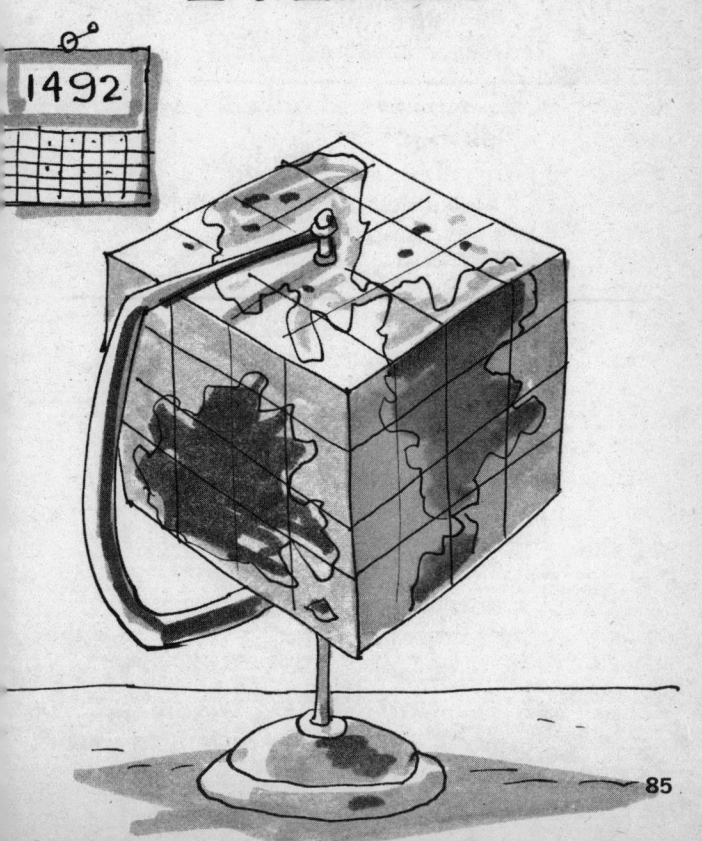

1651 B.C.
Moses Leads
His People To
The Red Sea

Sung to the tune of "Born Free"

Red Sea—
You better divide now!
It's time that you tried now!
Red Sea, please hear what I say!

Red Sea—
Just make a path narrow,
Or else that darn Pharoah
Is sure to get us today!

Red Sea—
I hope you come through, now,
Or else I will never be
In the Bible, you see!

Red Sea—
This thing I'm requestin'
Will mean Charlton Heston
Plays me. . . Red. . . Sea!

87

44 B.C.
Julius Caesar
Is Killed

Sung to the tune of
"Goodnight, Sweetheart"

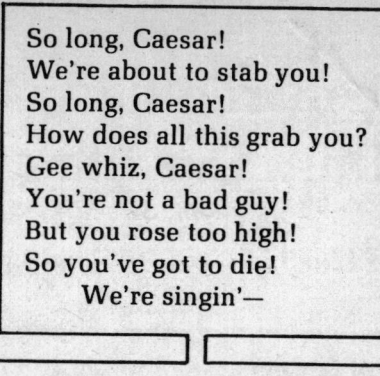

1506
Leonardo da Vinci Does Everything

Sung to the tune of
"There's No Business Like Show Business"

There's no genius but no genius
Like my genius, you see!
Go to Naples, Venice, Rome or Pisa--
You won't find a person half as smart;
People really dig my "Mona Lisa"—
They know that she's a
Great work of art!

There's no talent like my talent,
The whole world will agree!
I've designed machines in which a man can fly;
I've charted planets up in the sky;
I can even add, subtract and multiply;
Oh, gee!
I'm glad I'm me!

1587
Sir Walter Raleigh Introduces Tobacco To England

Sung to the tune of
"Hello, Dolly"

1805
Napoleon Decides To Conquer Europe

Sung to the tune of
"We'll Have Manhattan"

I'll conquer Russia!
Then all of Prussia
    I will win!
My troops will march right in
    Berlin!

I'll smash the Spanish
Until they vanish
    'neath the sea!
Then with artillery
I'll quickly fricassee
    Italy!

I'll clobber Britain!
It's just a sittin'
    duck for me!
I'll have their infantry
    for tea!

The map of Europe's a frosted bun
Made for Na-po-le-on!
I'll conquer Russia
'Cause war is so much fun!

1884
Sigmund Freud Discovers Psychoanalysis

Sung to the tune of
"(You're not sick) You're Just in Love"

I see toadstools in my dreams at night
Wearing neckties that are green and white!
When I pick them up, they die of fright!
    Please analyze!
    Please analyze!

I keep dreaming I'm a small giraffe,
Greeting folks who want my autograph!
When I sign my name, head-waiters laugh!
And then I break in half!
    Please analyze!

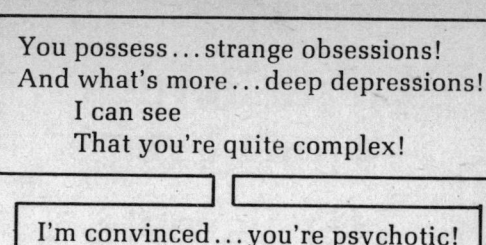

1892
Lizzie Borden
Knocks Off
Her Parents

Sung to the tune of
"Just One Of Those Things"

I was just doing my thing—
Just doing my special thing;
I grabbed an ax, and gave it a swing,
Just doing my thing;

I was just having some fun—
Just having some family fun;
I gave my folks one helluva fling,
Just doing my thing;

I was bored that day
With no games to play
When I gave my Mom a quick chop;
Then it seemed to me
She'd like company—
So I did likewise for Pop;

So, good-by, folks, and so long—
I'm sor-ry you can't hear this song;
You got the ax, true,
But I was just do-ing my thing!

A SONG TO SING WHILE WONDERING WHY YOU DON'T HAVE ANYTHING LEFT AT THE END OF THE YEAR

*In a bar!
At a show!
Ev'ry place
That I go!
There's one thing
That I know—
     They're taxing me!

Cars I rent!
Books I read!
Cans of glue!
Suits of tweed!
There's one thing
Guaranteed—
     They're taxing me!

For a seat
On a jet!
For a stereo set!
For Right Guard when I sweat!
You can bet
Tax they'll get—
     Yessiree!

Just you wait!
Pretty soon,
There'll be tax
On the moon!

When I've lived my last day,
And no longer can pay,
They will still find a way
     Of taxing me!

THE SOUND OF MURDER

CAST OF CHARACTERS

Louie Lasagna and his old-time, traditional mob of thugs, punks, goons and killers.

J. B. Tortoni and his new-wave crime syndicate of business executives and smooth operators.

107

* Dum-Dum DeCarlo, who comes from Miami—
Wally the Weasel and Light-Fingered Sammy—
Aspirin Artie, who's crazy from drugs—
These are a few of my favorite thugs!

*Sung to the tune of "My Favorite Things"

Izzy the Tailpipe, who holes up in Philly—
Elmo the Eel and his kid brother, Willy—
Homicide Harry, the sweetest of mugs—
These are the rest of my favorite thugs!

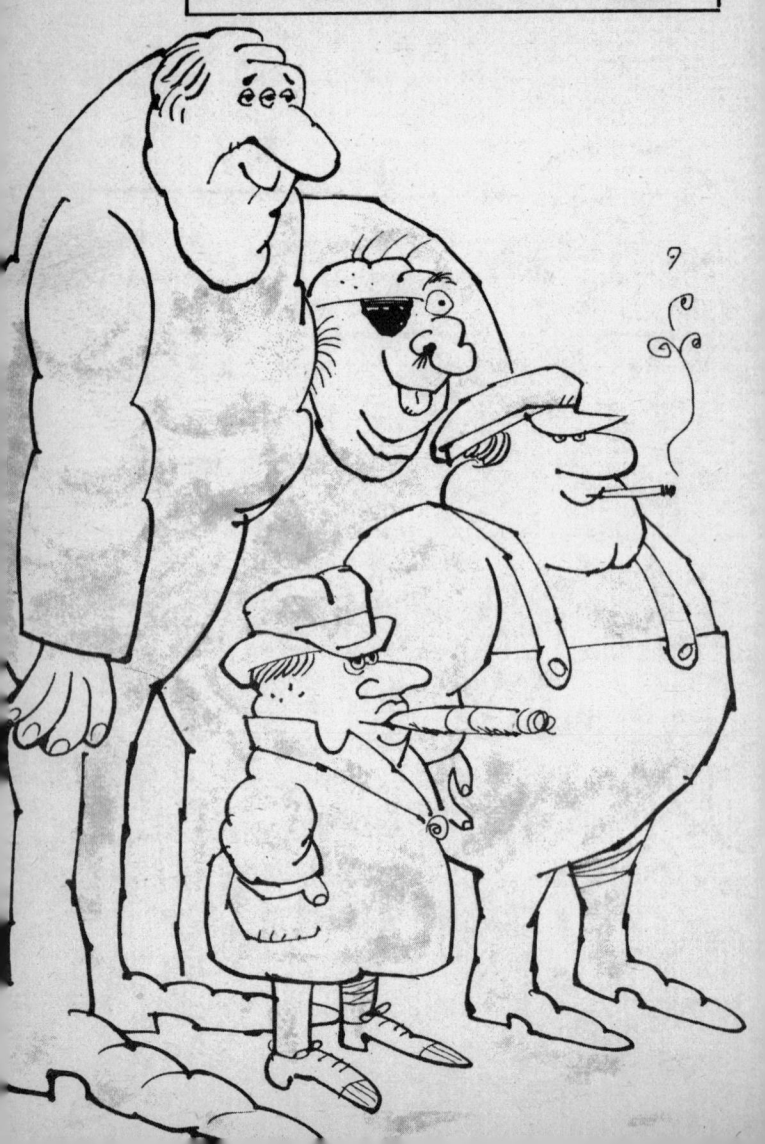

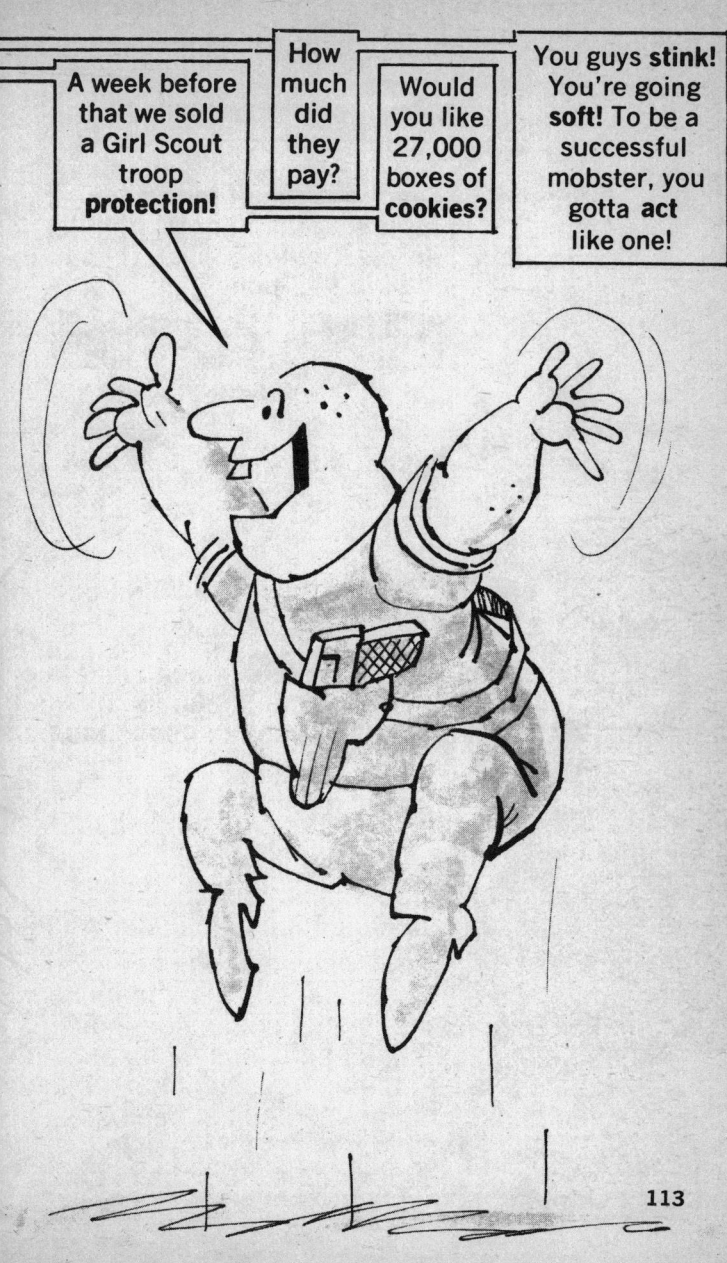

113

*Sung to the tune of "Climb Every Mountain"

*Sung to the tune of "The Sound of Music"

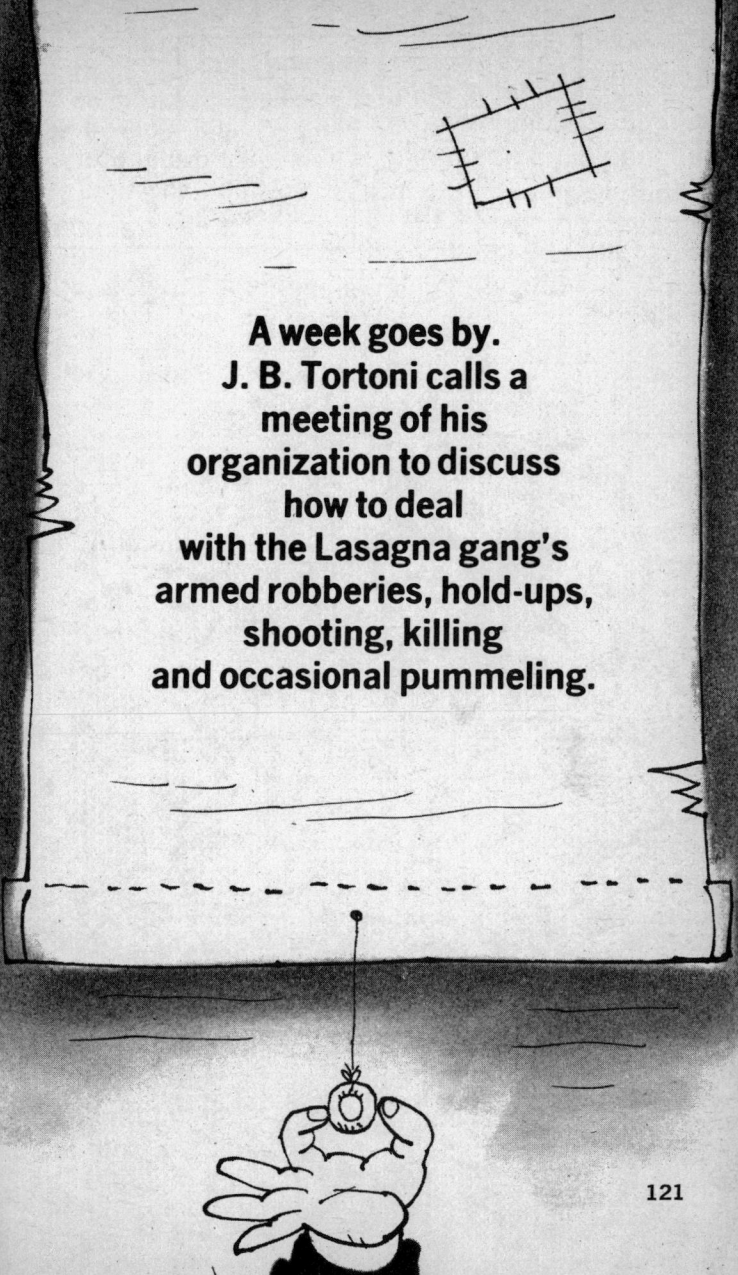

A week goes by.
J. B. Tortoni calls a
meeting of his
organization to discuss
how to deal
with the Lasagna gang's
armed robberies, hold-ups,
shooting, killing
and occasional pummeling.

123

127

133

134

136

We all agree his vi-o-lence is beastly;
Murder is crude and such a dreadful shame;
  The weapons that he employs
  Make such a shocking noise—
He's giving us all a most appalling name!
How do we solve the problem of Lasagna?
We've got to send him back from whence he came!

144

145

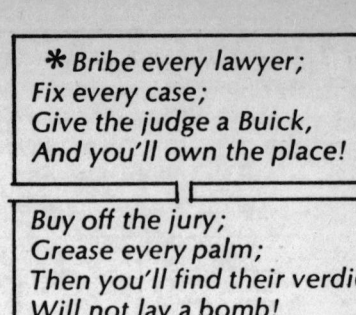

SONGS
FOR
DRIVING
ACROSS
AMERICA
BY

The Smog Of Los Angeles

Sung to the tune of "The Age Of Aquarius"

When the sun . . . is blotted out of sight,
And both your eyes . . . begin to burn,
And you . . . can't see the freeway
To make . . . that left-hand turn—

You know you're driving in
    The smog of Los Angeles!
    The smog of Los Angeles!
    Los Angeles! Los Angeles!

Traffic jams and drivers swearing!
Honking horns and sirens blaring!
Freeway signs obliterated!
Everyone exasperated!

There's no city worse to drive in!
You need luck to stay alive in
Los Angeles! Los Angeles!

Across The Foul Missouri

Sung to the tune of "Across The Wide Missouri"

From sewage plants comes an aroma
Along the foul Missouri!
With every gasp, we're in a coma!
   Let's drive
   While we're alive—
Across the foul Missouri!

With icky things the water's brimming
Across the foul Missouri!
Let's all give thanks that we're not swimming!
   Our car,
   Thank God, is far
Above the foul Missouri!

The air it reeks from dead fish drifting
Across the foul Missouri!
To make things worse, the wind is shifting!
   Alas!
   We're out of gas—
Above the foul Missouri!

At Night

Sung to the tune of "Tonight"

At night, at night,
You make great time at night;
At night there is no traffic or strain;
At night, at night,
It's great to drive at night
Till a truck looms ahead in your lane!

Up-tight,
You find his high-beams blind you,
While seven feet behind you
Another truck's in sight!

Dead-white with fright,
You quickly find a pray'r to recite—
At night!

AN ALL-PURPOSE SONG THAT YOU CAN CONSTRUCT ALL BY YOURSELF

Simply fill in the numbered blanks from the corresponding numbered lists on the next page, and you can make your own

ALL-INCLUSIVE DO-IT-YOURSELF "HELLO" SONG

Give my regards to _____(1)_____;

Remember me _____(2)_____;

Tell all the gang _____(3)_____

That I will soon be there;

Whisper of how I'm yearning

To _____(4)_____ with that _____(5)_____ throng;

Give my regards to _____(6)_____

And say that I'll be there ere long!

(1)	(2)
Broadway	to Herald Square
Phoenix	to Phil and Claire
Stockholm	at Joe's Men's Wear
Sing Sing	to Woodstock's Fair
Zelda	to Fred Astaire
Myron	while seeing "Hair"
Gimbel's	to Berkeley Square
Mother	to ev'ry square
Fido	though I don't care

(3)

on 42nd Street
in Yankee Stadium
in Boise, Idaho,
in Artie's Candy Store
I owe a bundle to
who roam the Bowery
in Ladies Underwear
who dig pornography
who've bought this stupid book

(4)	(5)	(6)
mingle	old-time	old Broadway
drink up	teen-age	Portland, Maine
fumfet	drunken	Charlie's Bar
freak out	Commie	all the cons
grovel	sex-starved	Fillmore East
bust heads	boring	Sidney's wife
make out	drug-crazed	Fang and Prince
slalom	White House	around the house
suffer	tone-deaf	William Gaines

SONGS
OF DOCTORS,
PATIENTS
AND
POOR HEALTH

DR. WILL HACKEM

Hello, Young Doctors

Sung to the tune of "Hello, Young Lovers"

Hello, young doctors,
Wherever you are;
Be wise and follow this pitch:
Don't set a bone till you've read through this verse;
Don't sew a single stitch!

Be sure, young doctors,
Whatever you do;
Be sure your patients are rich;
Don't check their pulse till you check through
    their purse;
Then there will be no hitch!

I know how you'll feel
When you see some schlemiel
Who has fractured his skull in a crash—
Forget your goodwill
And don't treat him until
He has paid beforehand with cash!

Be quick, young doctors,
Whatever you do;
Be quick in setting your fee;
Get all you can while they've got it to get;
You'll make a mint just like me;
You'll make a mint just like me, my lads,
You'll make a mint just like me!

The Transplant Patient's Hymn

Sung to the tune of "Love Is Blue"

New! New! My heart is new!
Straight from a man in Kalamazoo;
New! New! My kidney's new!
It's guaranteed till '72;
New! New! My liver's new!
If it gives out, a trade-in will do;
New! New! My stomach's new!
They had a sale—I could have bought two!

Late . . . last . . . year
When I went . . . in-sane—
I . . . just . . . shopped
For a slight-ly used brain!

New! New! My lungs are new!
So is my spleen, my pancreas, too!
New! New! I've so much new,
I'm a new man, but I'm not sure who!

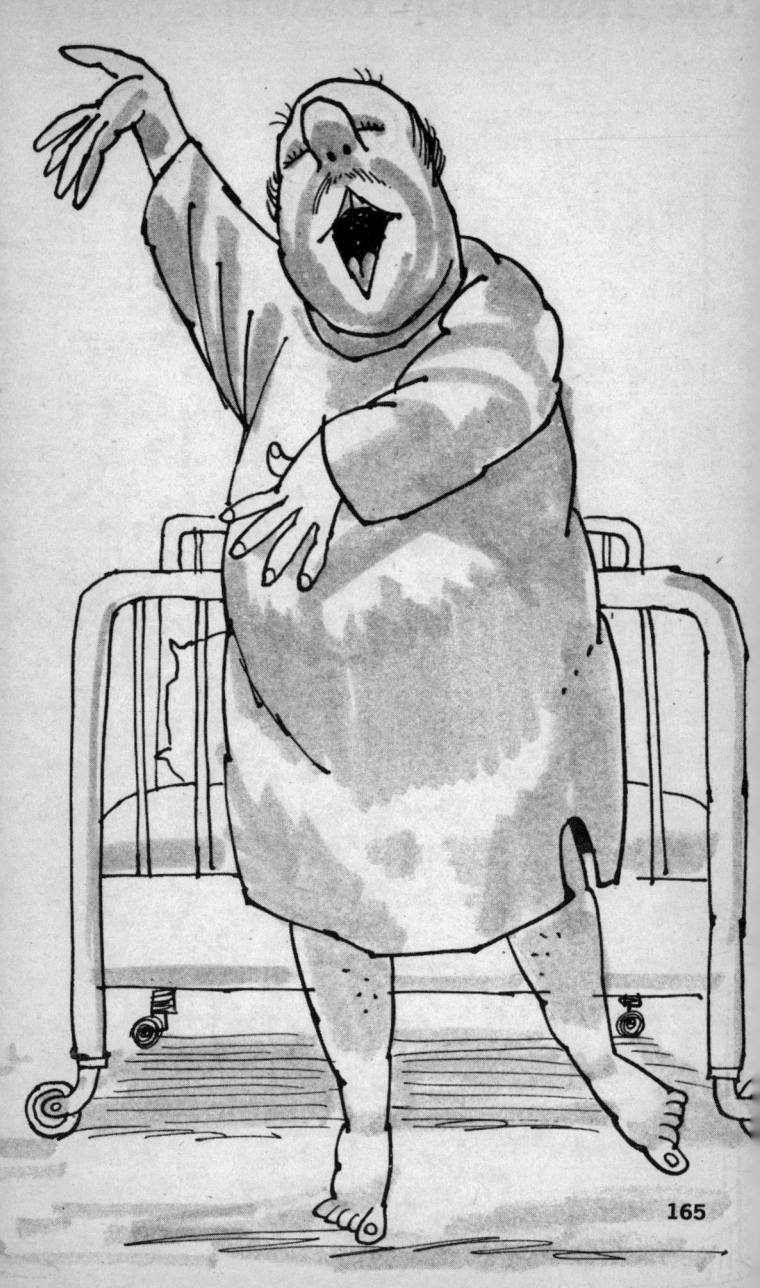

The Drug Company Rouser

Sung to the tune of "There Are Smiles"

We make pills
To stop your sneezing!

We make pills
To cure the shakes!

We make pills
To take when you feel rotten,
And you find your little
    tum-tum aches!

We make pills
To soothe you when you're
    nervous!

We make pills
That fill you with a glow!

But the pills
That we are really pushing
Are the pills at a buck a throw!

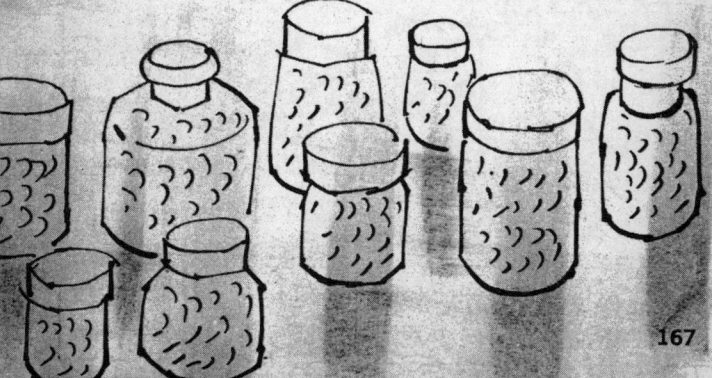

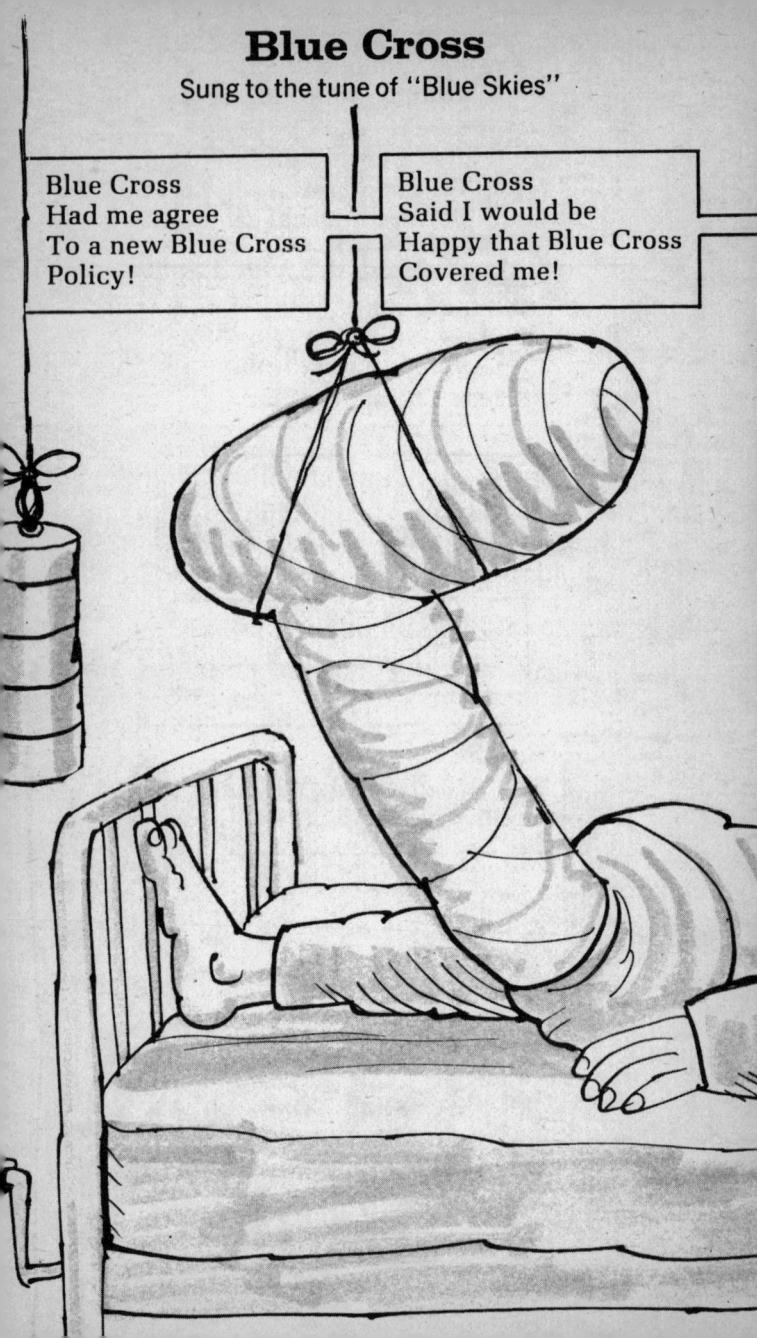

A SONG
REVEALING
THE BARE FACTS
OF
SHOW BUSINESS

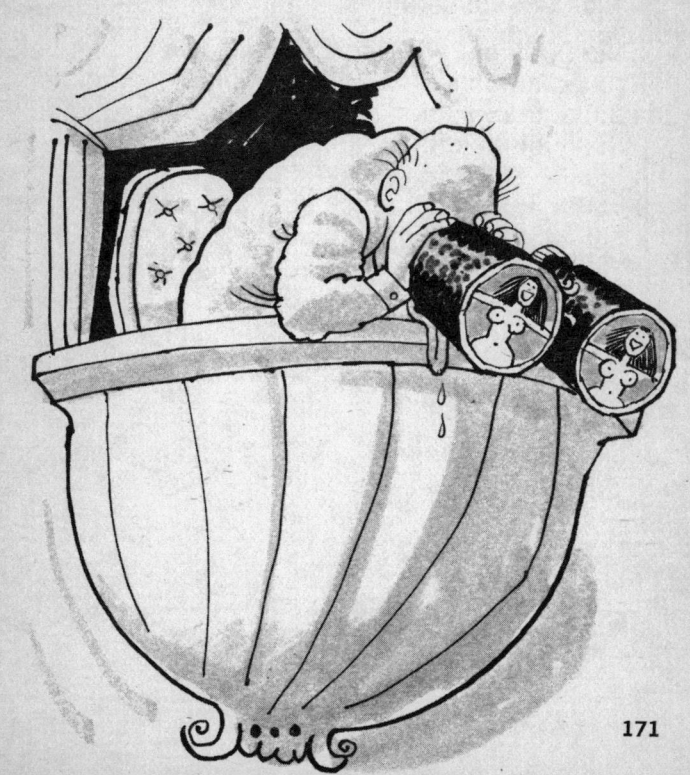

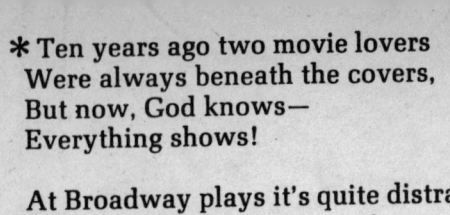

＊Ten years ago two movie lovers
Were always beneath the covers,
But now, God knows—
Everything shows!

At Broadway plays it's quite distracting
To see that the stars are acting
Without their clothes—
Everything shows!

Performers go nude today,
Act lewd today;
They're bare today
In "Hair" today,
And all the costumes that they wear today
Won't fill a bug's nose!

Next year our wigs we'll all be flipping
From Rowan and Martin stripping
Down to their toes—
Everything shows!

*Sung to the tune of "Anything Goes"

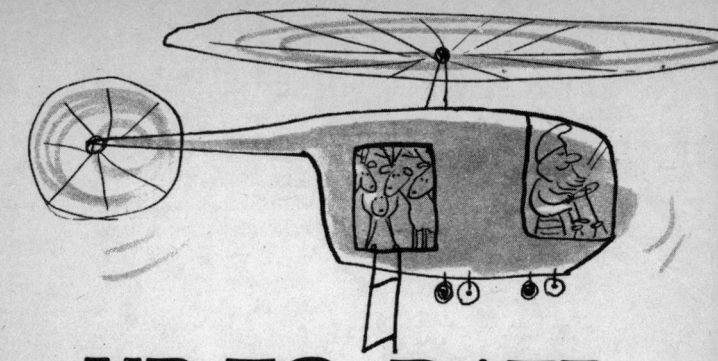

UP-TO-DATE CHRISTMAS SONGS

The Apartment Dweller's Yuletide Lament

Sung to the tune of
"Winter Wonderland"

Doorbells ring!
    It's the season;
And you know
    What's the reason:
There's someone out there
Who's after his share —
Sticking out his greedy little hand!

First to come
    Is the doorman;
He'll complain
    He's a poor man;
The janitor's next
On some weak pretext —
Sticking out his greedy little hand!

Then will come your super'ntendent's visit
    He will ring your doorbell loud and long;
You will open up an ask, "What is it?"
    He'll just smile and sing a Christmas song!

Later on,
    You'll get cash up
For the man
    Who picks trash up;
How nice they're all here
For one day a year —
Sticking out that greedy little hand!

ELEVATOR
NOT
WORKING

We The Men From Post Office Are

Sung to the tune of
"We Three Kings of Orient Are"

We're the men who carry great sacks
Full of Christmas cards on our backs;
    Schlepping, dragging,
    Shoulders sagging,
Till we fall in our tracks!
    Oh-h-h-h-h —
Cards for Herman, cards for Sue;
Cards with six cents postage due;
    Ever-sending,
    Never-ending,
Cards we'd like to tear in two!

Fill The Bars

Sung to the tune of
"Deck the Halls"

Fill the bars with Christmas drinking!
Fa la la la la—la la la la!
See the people getting stinking!
Fa la la la la — la la la la!
Though their brains are half-corroded —
Fa la la—la la la—la la la!
Still they'll try to drive home loaded!
Fa la la la la la — la la la la!

See the busy intersection!
　　Fa la la la la — la la la la!
Here come cars from each direction!
　　Fa la la la la — la la la la!
See the pile-up when they're meeting!
　　Fa la la—la la la—la la la!
What a novel Christmas greeting!
　　Fa la la la la — la la la la!

Hear the sounds of sirens blowing!
Fa la la la la — la la la la!
See the Yuletide death toll growing!
Fa la la la la — la la la la!
That's the fate of drunken drivers!
Fa la la—la la la—la la la!
Sing this song to their survivors!
Fa la la la la — la la la la!

Christmas Bills

Sung to the tune of
"Jingle Bells"

Christmas bills —
Christmas bills —
    Pil-ed on the floor;
Every day the mailman comes
    to bring a dozen more!
        Oh!
Christmas bills —
Christmas bills —
    How the stores will swear!
When they soon discover that
    my bank account is bare!

Dashing off the checks —
  All in great amounts —
Mailing them today —
  Knowing they will bounce!
Bill collectors come —
  Notify my boss —
Now they get my salary —
  My life's a total loss!

Oh-h-h-h-h —
Christmas bills —
Christmas bills —
Making me lament;
Now I'm up against the wall
from all those gifts I sent!
Oh!
Christmas bills —
Christmas bills —
I'll go broke and then,
When next Christmas rolls around
I'll do it all again!

The Christmas Of Jackie Onassis

Sung to the tune of
"The 12 Days of Christmas"

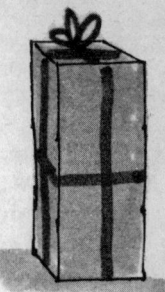

On the First day of Christmas
Onassis gave to me —
　　The Statue of Li-i-berty!

On the Second day of Christmas
Onassis gave to me —
　　Ni-agara Falls
　　And the Statue of Li-i-berty!

On the Third day of Christmas
Onassis gave to me —
　　Plymouth Rock,
　　Ni-agara Falls
　　And the Statue of Li-i-berty!

On the Fourth day of Christmas
Onassis gave to me —
　　Fifth Avenue,
　　Plymouth Rock,
　　Ni-agara Falls
　　And the Statue of Li-i-berty!

On the Fifth day of Christmas
Onassis gave to me —
    The New York Mets,
    Fi-fth Avenue,
    Plymouth Rock,
    Ni-i-agara Falls
    And the Statue of Li-i-berty!

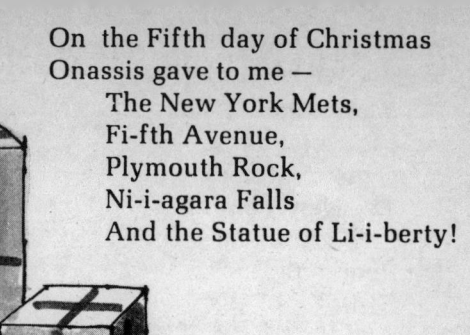

On the Sixth day of Christmas
Onassis gave to me —
    General Motors,
    The New York Mets,
    Fi-fth Avenue,
    Plymouth Rock,
    Ni-i-agara Falls
    And the Statue of Li-i-berty!

On the Seventh day of Christmas
Onassis gave to me —
    Rio de Janeiro,
    General Motors,
    The New York Mets,
    Fi-fth Avenue,
    Plymouth Rock,
    Ni-i-agara Falls
    And the Statue of Li-i-berty!

On the Eighth day of Christmas
Onassis gave to me —
 Westminster Abbey,
 Rio de Janeiro,
 General Motors,
 The New York Mets,
 Fi-fth Avenue,
 Plymouth Rock,
 Ni-i-agara Falls
 And the Statue of Li-i-berty!

On the Ninth day of Christmas
Onassis gave to me —
 Fort Knox, Kentucky,
 Westminster Abbey,
 Rio de Janeiro,
 General Motors,
 The New York Mets,
 Fi-fth Avenue,
 Plymouth Rock,
 Ni-i-agara Falls
 And the Statue of Li-i-berty!

On the Tenth day of Christmas
Onassis gave to me —
    Pablo Picasso,
    Fort Knox, Kentucky,
    Westminster Abbey,
    Rio de Janeiro,
    General Motors,
    The New York Mets,
    Fi-fth Avenue,
    Plymouth Rock,
    Ni-i-agara Falls
And the Statue of Li-i-berty!

On the Eleventh day of Christmas
Onassis gave to me —
    Communist Asia,
    Pablo Picasso,
    Fort Knox, Kentucky,
    Westminster Abbey,
    Rio de Janeiro,
    General Motors,
    The New York Mets,
    Fi-fth Avenue,
    Plymouth Rock,
    Ni-i-agara Falls
And the Statue of Li-i-berty!

On the Twelfth day of Christmas
Onassis gave to me —
Two weeks' allowance,
Communist Asia,
Pablo Picasso,
Fort Knox, Kentucky,
Westminster Abbey,
Rio de Janeiro,
General Motors,
The New York Mets,
Fi-fth Avenue,
Plymouth Rock,
Ni-i-agara Falls
And the Statue of Li-i-berty!

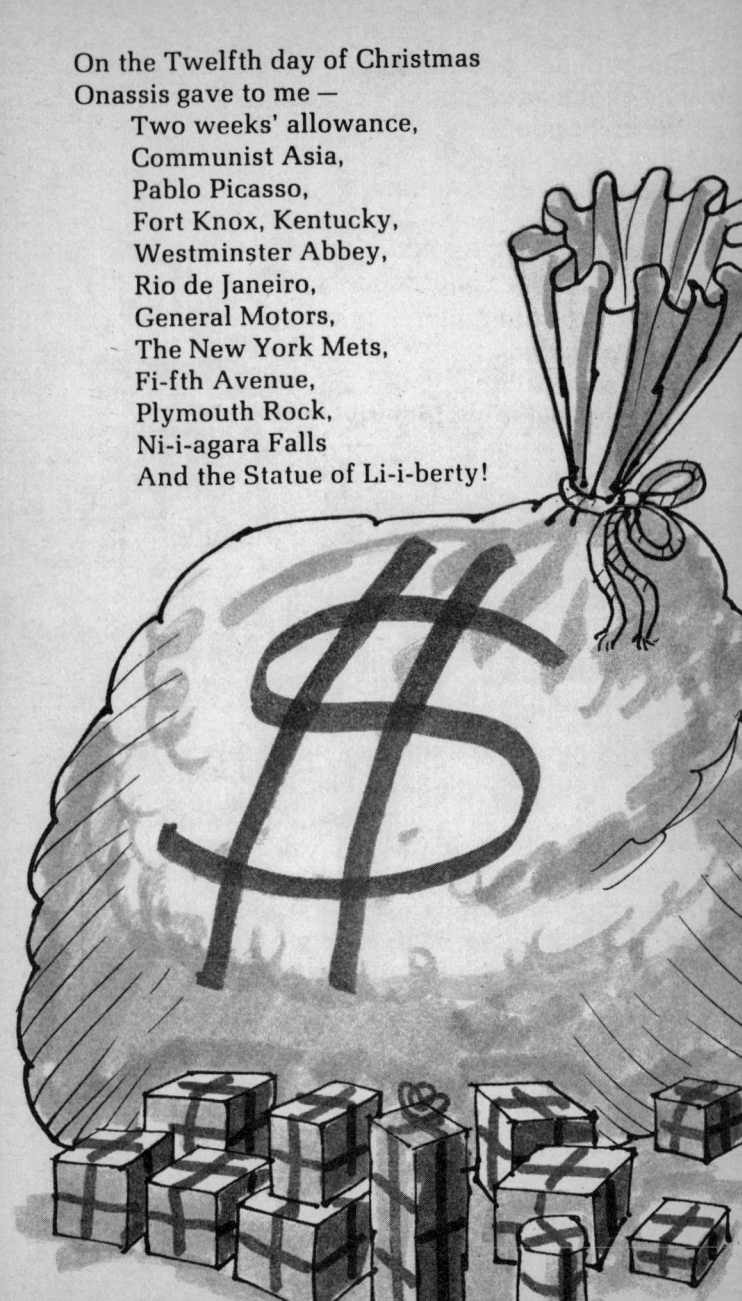